big brands

MINECRAFT

Chris Martin

WAYLAND

contents

gaming becomes big business

The first ever video game developed was the "Cathode Ray Tube Amusement Device". It was a missile launch game, programmed on a piece of scientific equipment by physicists Thomas T. Goldsmith Jr. and Estle Ray Mann in 1947. They created it for fun, with little idea of the potential revenue that gaming would one day generate!

In the decades since the invention of the first game, the industry has exploded. New hardware, such as Atari's home gaming consoles, developed in the 1970s, have led to some advances. Others have been the result of individual games capturing the public's imagination: for example *Super Mario Brothers*, which brought arcade gaming into the home, or *World of Warcraft*, which allowed millions of people to play and build worlds together online. Today it is estimated that the global games industry is worth in the region of $83 billion a year, with online and mobile games making up more than half of this.

The best-selling video game of all time is *Tetris*, a basic block game. It has shifted an incredible 143 million copies since 1984. But at number three on the list is a game that has only been in existence since 2009: *Minecraft*.

New affordable hardware led to a revolution in video gaming.

Business Matters
Revenue

Revenue is the money that comes into a company or organization as a result of its business ventures.

Mario Brothers was one of the first games to move from the arcade into the home.

Minecraft is the work of small games studio called Mojang, based in Stockholm, in Sweden. It has become an international phenomenon – in 2014 it was estimated that five people bought the game every second – and enabled Mojang to build a brand covering games, books and toys, based around a dedicated community of loyal fans. This book looks at *Minecraft's* extraordinary story, how it has been so successful, so fast, and at what the future might hold for both the company and the game.

> **When you go online, you can build whatever you want in a space. The physical bit of building is so much easier than the real world because *Minecraft* is all in blocks so everything fits. It's really exciting to be able to make so much in a small amount of time. The sky's the limit.**
>
> Theo Gabb, 12, *Minecraft* fan

Minecraft sold over one million copies in just two years.

from Minecraft to Microsoft

Minecraft is one of the world's best-known gaming brands. Its success has allowed Mojang, the company created to develop and market it, to grow at incredible speed. The first version of *Minecraft* was made available on developer Markus Persson's website in 2009, costing just €15.00. In 2010, Persson and games designer Jakob Porsér founded Mojang in Stockholm, Sweden.

At the beginning of 2011, the third co-founder of Mojang, Carl Manneh, joined the company as its CEO, finding offices for the company, and employing developers. This took employee numbers to seven. In August 2011, Mojang published a game called *Cobalt*, developed by another small, Swedish games company called Oxeye Game Studios. This was followed by *Minecraft: Pocket Edition*, which was developed especially to be played on mobiles. By November 2011, *Minecraft* had sold a million copies.

In March 2012, Mojang's revenue hit $80 million per year, a figure that was boosted in May when *Minecraft* was released on Xbox 360. Also in 2012,

Business Matters
Developer

Developers are computer programmers who work on code for games, software or websites on the World Wide Web.

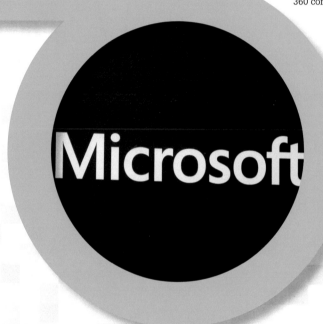

Minecraft was a huge success on Microsoft's Xbox 360 console.

Building the Brand
The Mojang Logo

A logo is a visual icon used to represent the company's mark to their customers and suppliers. Some examples of famous logos are the apple used by Apple, or the tick found on Nike products. The Mojang logo is a square, hollow object with a flame on one corner. Some people argue that it's a dragon shooting fire or a square apple (because everything in *Minecraft* is square). Others say that it's a sewing machine perhaps because 'mojang' in Swedish means gadget. Markus Persson has tweeted on the subject but gave little away, saying the logo was "just abstract, but it kind of looks like a sewing machine." In other words, next time you see it, make up your own mind! Threads on some *Minecraft* fan forums are devoted to debating what the Mojang logo is. Suggestions include an anteater, a hole dug into a hill and even an abstract rhino!

the first *Minecraft* Lego set was released, as was *Scrolls*, another Mojang game. By December 2012, 15 million copies of *Minecraft* had been sold on Mac, Windows, Linux, Xbox, Android and iOS. At the start of 2013, Mojang's numbers had swelled to a grand total of 37 employees. By June 2014, *Minecraft* had sold 54 million copies worldwide and in September, the gaming world was stunned when computer giant Microsoft announced it was going to buy Mojang for an incredible $2.5 billion.

Business Matters

What is a brand?

The word 'brand' derives from the symbol burned onto an animal's side with a branding iron to identify them as a farmer's property. It is a term used in advertising and marketing to describe the assets that distinguish a company, its products and activities from another company's in the eyes of its customers; for example Pepsi from Coca Cola.

Some fans of the *Minecraft* brand enjoy dressing up as characters from the game.

Markus Persson

founder of Mojang and creator of *Minecraft*

The popularity of his creation made Markus Persson a gaming superstar.

Persson, also known online as 'Notch', was born in Stockholm in 1979. He began programming at the age of seven and produced his first game at the age of eight. After leaving school, he worked for games developer King.com, where he wrote the first version of *Minecraft* in his spare time. In September 2010, Persson founded Mojang AB with his best friend Jakob Porsér to develop *Minecraft*. Persson has become a celebrity in his own right, appearing on chat shows and talking frequently on social media. He has remained down to earth, despite his success. On *Minecraft* he says: "I still feel a bit like it's just this small game I made at home. It's so weird to have all these things happen."

a unique approach

Unlike many big brands, Mojang's founders had a very special approach to business, and the development of games. The people behind *Minecraft* were computer programmers, not businessmen. They are used to sharing their skills and their work on the Internet with other developers so they can work together to make their games better.

As a result, Mojang has improved *Minecraft* and its other games by listening to their community of fans. They actively encourage fans to get involved in enhancing their games – for example, by creating new artwork, or even building applications that run in the game. However, Mojang still needs to keep control over how its games are used, and especially who can make money from them. They publish a set of guidelines defining what is and isn't allowed, covering three key things:

Their name – *this is both the name of the company and the individual names of their games.*
Their brands – *the related logos and distinctive design features of their games.*
Their assets – *the code, graphics and sounds of their games. These are the building blocks of a tech business.*

Although the language used in Mojang's brand guidelines seems relaxed, it is still a legal document. It makes a clear distinction between fan activities, such as making videos, and anything done by other companies for profit. There is a practical point to this. If there was no control then anyone could sell games that looked like Mojang games but weren't as good.

Minecraft
in your pocket

Technology allows people to access their favourite programs and games through PCs, home consoles, tablets, laptops and smartphones, all of which need different software to operate. While there are some obvious differences between these devices (for example, the size of the screen) people using them still expect all their favourite programs to work in the same way. As a result, tech companies have to create lots of versions of software so that their customers can use it on any device of their choosing.

Mojang has been really successful in offering *Minecraft* on multiple devices and adapting it to match each different type of software. Originally *Minecraft* was a PC game downloaded from the Internet and, in fact, it still is. Mojang sells the PC version itself – and takes all the money – on its website. However Mojang has also

A boy plays on an early PlayStation model.

Business Matters
Platforms

A platform is the name given to the device or basic code on which a game runs. This may be unique to a single device, like Apple's Mac OS running on an iMac computer, or shared, like Google's Android OS that runs on a variety of mobile phones and tablets.

Minecraft: Pocket Edition is slightly different to the full game to make it easier to play on a small screen.

gone into partnership with other companies to make the game available on more than nine other platforms, encompassing nearly every software system from Apple to Sony.

By June 2014, Mojang had sold more than 54 million copies of *Minecraft*, only 16 million of which were the original PC version. In 2012, their partnership with Microsoft led to the launch of the game on Xbox 360, meaning *Minecraft* could be played by people who did not own a PC. More than 13 million copies of *Minecraft* for Xbox 360 were sold in two years.

However, these figures were nothing compared to *Minecraft's* move to mobile devices. *Minecraft: Pocket Edition* was launched in 2011. It could be played on phones and tablets, and was sold at a slightly cheaper price. *Minecraft: Pocket Edition* remains one of the top paid-for iPhone apps, and has sold about 22 million copies on the Apple IOS and Google Android.

> " The gift was giving people a world to play with. *Minecraft* trusts in people's ability to find their own entertainment... It is a glimpse into a new world of digital entertainment. "
>
> **Peter Molyneux, Games Designer and creator of Populus**

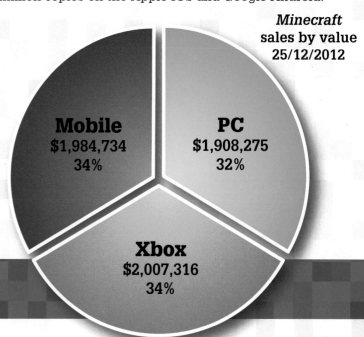

Minecraft sales by value 25/12/2012

Mobile $1,984,734 34%

PC $1,908,275 32%

Xbox $2,007,316 34%

what is Minecraft?

Minecraft is a first-person "sandbox" game. This means the game offers individual players a whole world to interact with as they want, a bit like a child in a sandpit. In gaming, this often means players are able to adapt the game's software to create their own playing experience, for example by changing backgrounds or levels.

The virtual world in *Minecraft* lets players collect (mine) 3D blocks to build (craft) things. Players can create houses, weave clothing, grow crops and even mix up spells and potions. The *Minecraft* world – like the real world – has day and night, bad weather, mountains, plains and jungles. It is full of animals and plants that you can farm or kill for food. It is also populated by monsters such as creepers, zombies and giant spiders, so players must create weapons to survive.

Players can choose between four levels of difficulty, Peaceful, Easy, Normal and Hard. There are also four game modes:

Creative mode – no monsters and unlimited resources
Survival mode – where monsters will try to kill you, and you need to collect all your own resources
Hard-core mode – like Survival but with just one life
Spectator mode – where you can fly around and watch others.

Business Matters
Code

A set of instructions or statements that make up a computer program. Like a spoken language, computer languages use different combinations of words to describe what they do. *Minecraft* is written in a language called Java.

Minecraft's open code base has led to its use by ICT teachers in schools.

Tools, Weapons & Armour

Leather Pants

Clear Quick Select   What's This?

Playing online can add a whole new dimension to the game. By connecting to other players in a shared world, you can share your creations or access special software modifications, which come in two forms:

Mods – code that changes the way the game behaves.

Resource packs – images and sounds that change the way the game looks.

Minecraft's software is built to allow advanced players to hack the game and build incredible machines in the virtual world, from working computers to playable guitars. It is this ability to allow people to use their imaginations that has made *Minecraft* such a success with players. The creativity of the game, its relatively simple format and its block-like, 8-bit graphics have led many to describe it as a kind of online Lego.

Gamers can download mods to change the way *Minecraft* plays.

Building the Brand
Minecraft Lego

A successful brand will be approached by lots of companies to create a product to benefit them both. Mojang felt that the similarity between *Minecraft* and Lego, both creative, block-based games, was too good to pass up. They approached Lego through its open innovation website, Lego CUUSOO (now Lego Ideas), to create *Minecraft*-themed sets. The website allows anyone to submit a concept for Lego to consider. Lego fans can vote on the ones they want to see made and, if a project draws 10,000 votes, Lego gets to work. The *Minecraft* project achieved this in 48 hours, and the first set, 21102 Micro World, was released in 2012. Mojang receive one per cent of the proceeds and donate the money to charity. The success of the first Lego set has led to 10 more being created, including set 21113 The Cave.

Programmers at work in Mojang's office in Stockholm, Sweden.

Business Matters
Copyright

Copyright is a legal term that is used to describe how the law protects the rights of the creator of a piece of work or creative concept. This law ensures that the holder of the copyright will be the only person who can earn money from their idea.

branching out

Scrolls was inspired by real-world card trading games.

Typically in the gaming world, a games studio either creates games or publishes them on the behalf of other studios. Mojang does both. In addition to *Minecraft*, it is responsible for two further games.

Launched in 2012, *Scrolls* is a turn-based strategy game, similar to offline trading card games such as *Magic: the Gathering*. Played on a battlefield that is a bit like a chessboard, players can earn or buy cards that are then used to summon magic to destroy their opponent's pieces (or idols). The first player to destroy three of their opponent's idols wins.

Despite being an original concept, Mojang was sued by a rival games company, Bethesda Softworks, who claimed the name *Scrolls* could be confused with its successful *Elder Scrolls* series. The lawsuit was eventually dropped when both parties agreed not to compete with each other.

Cobalt, launched in 2011, is based around a robot called Metalface. The game has various multi-player features, as well as the ability to let players change its levels. Unlike *Scrolls*, which was built by their own developers, Mojang is only the publisher of *Cobalt*, not its creator.

Daniel Rosenfeld
composer of the music for Minecraft

Daniel Rosenfeld (also known as C418) is a German electronic musician. His unique sounds were used to add atmosphere to game play in *Minecraft*, as well as various sound effects such as monster noises. The recruitment of Rosenfeld was an example of how Markus Persson assembled the talent behind *Minecraft* using the Internet. Persson first met Rosenfeld in an online chat room devoted to music. He shared the game he was working on (*Minecraft*) and Rosenfeld shared his music. Rosenfeld has released two official *Minecraft* soundtracks. *Minecraft – Volume Alpha* and *Minecraft – Volume Beta* both feature music from the game.

Slum housing in Kibera, in Kenya, where *Minecraft* has been used for social good.

Business Matters
Corporate Social Responsibility (CSR)

CSR refers to a company's approach to how they do business. CSR policies may cover a company's ethics, or mean they develop areas of their business that have a positive social impact, for example by working with charities.

giving something back

The *Minecraft* brand has made a huge amount of money for Mojang's staff, the companies who sell their merchandise and the retailers who sell the games. However, Mojang also use their products and the skills of their team to help others.

The 'Humble Bundle' is a package of video games sold online every year to raise money for charity. Mojang contributed games to the Humble Bundle in 2012 and 2013. In 2012, an event named "Mojam" saw Mojang developers create a game called *Catacomb Snatch* for the Humble Bundle in a non-stop 60-hour hackathon. The game raised $450,000 for various charities. In 2013, an expanded Mojang team created four games: *Battle Frogs*, *Endless Nuclear Kittens*, *Nuclear Pizza War* and *Nuke the Dinosaurs*, raising a further $510,000 for the charities.

Also in 2013, Mojang joined forces with the United Nations to become the main sponsor of Block by Block. Block by Block is part of the UN's Human Settlements Programme (UN-Habitat), a series of international projects to try to create better cities around the world. The first project focused on Kibera, in Kenya, where young people used *Minecraft* to redesign the public spaces where they lived.

Such projects have a double value for Mojang. Firstly, it is good for their image to be seen doing charity work, and helping others. Secondly, as a business led by developers, Mojang values projects that creatively challenge and engage its staff.

Building the Brand
Minecon

Minecon is the annual convention held for fans of *Minecraft*. It has its roots in Minecraftcon, an informal convention of just 50 people in Washington in 2010. In 2011, the first official Minecon was held at the Mandalay Bay resort in Las Vegas and included discussion panels, building contests and costume shows. In 2012, Minecon was held in Paris and was used in a more traditional way, to celebrate the success of the game on Xbox 360, and to announce new software updates. By 2013, unofficial Minecons or "Virtual Minecons" had begun to spring up online to support the real event. The 2013 Minecon in Florida sold out in minutes after it was announced on Mojang's YouTube channel, attracting some 7,500 attendees.

Minecraft fans watch a talk by Markus Persson at Minecon 2012 in Paris.

conquering

Egmont is an ideal partner for companies like Rovio and Mojang. As a children's publisher, it understands how to make its books as appealing as the games themselves.

the world of books

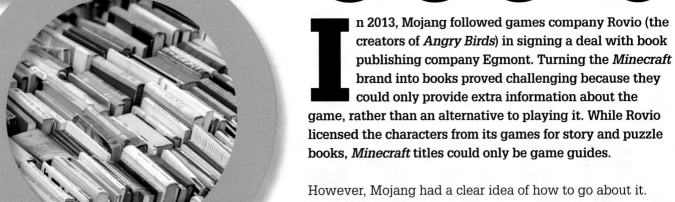

In 2013, Mojang followed games company Rovio (the creators of *Angry Birds*) in signing a deal with book publishing company Egmont. Turning the *Minecraft* brand into books proved challenging because they could only provide extra information about the game, rather than an alternative to playing it. While Rovio licensed the characters from its games for story and puzzle books, *Minecraft* titles could only be game guides.

However, Mojang had a clear idea of how to go about it. The books targeted both new players and existing fans, and were written by the Mojang team, rather than ghostwriters, to ensure accuracy. The first five books: *Minecraft: Essential Handbook, Minecraft: Redstone Handbook, Minecraft: Annual 2014, Minecraft: Combat Handbook* and *Minecraft: Construction Handbook* published in 2014, and topped the children's book charts. The official *Minecraft Handbook* went on to sell 1 million copies.

Egmont sold more than 8 million copies of their *Minecraft* titles in 24 countries, and the books' success meant they expanded their *Minecraft* range. The original five books have been joined by the *Minecraft Annual*, featuring step-by-step instructions for building and hints from the experts, and *Blockopedia*, an exhaustive *Minecraft* encyclopedia featuring information on all 112 blocks in the game.

Business Matters
Licensing

Licensing is renting the use of a company's brand. It is managed by a contract between the owner of the brand and a company that wants to use it on their own products. Typically these contracts will specify how the brand can be used, in which countries, and for what period of time. Mojang licenses its *Minecraft* brand to a range of items, from T-shirts and plush toys to jewellery. However the company has a very clear policy on licensing; namely, that it should never become more important than the game.

> **If you look at where kids are choosing to spend their time, they are moving away from the TV… to the tablets and to other gaming elements. We have moved our publishing attention to that whole genre.**
>
> Emma Cairn-Smith, Licensing
> Director of Egmont

Minecraft merch

In the marketing world, the term 'merchandising', or 'merch', describes when a brand from one product is used to sell another. For example, a brand owner might license names, logos or images to a toy manufacturer or a clothing company. Licensing a brand is beneficial to a manufacturer because branded items sell better than non-branded ones do.

Merchandising is used on everything from T-shirts to children's cereal, and for the owners of a brand it can be a profitable source of income. As long as the products don't damage the brand by being poor quality or dangerous, the owners do nothing but collect fees.

Business Matters
Prototype

The first working version of a new product, developed to test whether or not it works. Prototypes often go through several stages of modification and refinement before the final product is reached.

Minecraft merchandise is a key part of the experience for fans.

Often the fans of a brand will actively want some kind of merchandise, and *Minecraft* fans are no exception. However Mojang was keen that any *Minecraft* merch be of high quality and – as always – support the game experience rather than replace it.

The answer came when a clothing company called J!NX presented a prototype T-shirt that read 'I pork chop *Minecraft*'. By using a familiar item from the game – a pork chop – J!NX was able to show it understood the playful nature of the *Minecraft* brand, and the Mojang team knew they were a company they wanted to work with. Now J!NX sell a range of *Minecraft* merch, from hoodies to cuddly creatures from the game, in an official, dedicated *Minecraft* store online.

Jakob Porsér
co-founder and game designer at Mojang

Porsér was Markus Persson's righthand man on the development of *Minecraft* and is also credited as lead designer on *Scrolls*. It was Porsér who defined the easy-going production process at Mojang. He wrote on the Mojang website: "There's no design doc, but there are two lists: one for bugs, and one for features I want to add but think I might forget."

Porsér previously worked with Persson at King.com and it was while they were there that the two also began work on *Scrolls*. While *Scrolls* has been somewhat dwarfed by the success of *Minecraft*, it continues to build a small but loyal following. Like Persson, Porsér is a keen blogger and tweeter, and helped to keep *Minecraft* fans in touch with all things Mojang.

a world united
the minecraft community

Children in Michigan, USA do papercraft inspired by *Minecraft* at a craft fair.

In addition to creating the *Minecraft* game, Mojang has built a unique community of players online. Much of this is based around thousands of *Minecraft* fan videos posted on YouTube and Twitch TV, but the relationship also relies on constant direct communication between the Mojang team and fans.

Mojang estimate that the team broadcast around 100 messages a day via Twitter, the company blog, personal staff blogs and other social media such as Reddit and Tumblr. Markus Persson's posts were so popular that he gained a cult following under his online name, Notch. His personal messages gave fans a genuine sense that they knew what Notch was up to, and what he thought about all things gaming, music and Mojang.

Minecraft's community is an amazing marketing resource, enabling the company to sell more products; but it is also a practical way to manage a business built around a product that is constantly changing. Mojang can communicate with players directly to explain company decisions and bugs in games releases, and even to collect ideas for new features.

Business Matters
EULA

An End-User License Agreement is a legal agreement between a games publisher and someone who buys their product. Commonly this contract covers both the right of the player to copy and install the game and protects the publisher's copyright.

Independent networks of servers have made playing *Minecraft* with others part of the game.

Unlike a regular company, that might keep their customers informed about what's going on through press releases, Mojang can keep its customers up to date with company decisions as they happen.

As well as running on individual PCs and consoles, *Minecraft* can run as a multiplayer game that allows players to collaborate in shared worlds. These worlds require a lot of computer power and must be run on machines called servers. Unusually, Mojang allows anyone to create a *Minecraft* server, which means that *Minecraft* has been able to spread massively online, without the company needing to invest in hardware.

These servers must abide by certain rules stated in an End-User License Agreement (EULA) agreement with Mojang. The rules allow anyone hosting a *Minecraft* server to take donations and fees for that service. However, they cannot charge for enhanced access nor can they sell items that give players an unfair advantage in the game. Operations like HiveMC, Mineplex, Shotbow or Hypixel can attract well over a million

players every month. Often they employ their own developers to run the servers, protect against attack, moderate the environment and create new content.

Some of these services have an educational aim, such as Minecraft Edu that supports the use of the game in schools. However the reality is that most of them compete with each other for customers by offering packages (or "ranks") including additional extras that can affect gameplay. For years Mojang ignored this, but in 2014 they decided to enforce the agreement and clamp down on the sale of such extras.

This issue presents a quandary for Mojang. *Minecraft* servers bring the game to millions of dedicated players and contribute to its popularity by creating new worlds, mini-games and communities. However Mojang does not benefit from the money they make. Mojang says they just want to make sure that access to these servers is not charged and that gameplay remains fair. The server owners say that the new rules will drive them out of business.

Minecraft on YouTube

One of the most unusual aspects of the success of *Minecraft* has been its extraordinary success on YouTube. The thousands of videos created by *Minecraft* fans on the channel serve to bind the community together. Some fans even make money from their videos thanks to the revenue created by advertising.

For *Minecraft* players, YouTube videos are an essential part of playing the game. There are tutorials, footage of people playing, demonstrations of new mods and even comedy films made using characters and sets created in the game. Many of the people who create the videos have become celebrities in their own right. SkythekidRS, CupQuake and CaptainSparklez have all made a name for themselves on YouTube. From Mojang's point of view these videos are the equivalent of millions of dollars in paid advertising and technical support. Not surprisingly, they tend to promote and celebrate this phenomenon.

Carl Manneh
co-founder and former CEO (Chief Executive Officer) of Mojang

Manneh founded the Swedish photo album start up jAlbum, to help people share their skiing shots, and met Markus Persson when he hired him as a web developer. Persson was already working on the first version of *Minecraft* and soon left to develop the game. When Persson decided to set up a games studio, he called Manneh to ask if he knew anyone who could run the business side of company. Manneh volunteered himself. Manneh ran the company up until its sale in 2014. So many people wanted to work with Mojang that he said his role was to act as a "big filter", adding: "The most common word I say is 'no'."

Business Matters
Structuring the company

Corporate structure is how a company organizes its staff and activities. This means creating departments and defining roles for the people who run them. Usually there is also a CEO (Chief Executive Officer) who leads the organisation and a board of Directors to set its broad policies.

Minecraft celebrity CupQuake attends a film premiere in Los Angeles.

Microsoft founder
Bill Gates.

Vu Bui
Chief Operating Officer (COO) of Mojang

The COO is responsible for the daily operation of a company. Bui's appointment shows how quickly Mojang has moved from being a group of friends coding together to a company that needs proper business structures to help it to run efficiently. However, Bui's background is unconventional for a COO. He is an American photographer and cinematographer living in Stockholm, and he still works as a filmmaker and teacher.

Bui controls licensing very tightly. He requires any potential licensee to display an in-depth of knowledge of how Mojang approach their work, why they make the products they do and the importance of their community.

the future of Mojang

In 2014 it was announced that software giant Microsoft was buying Mojang for an incredible $2.5 billion. While sales of *Minecraft* have been impressive, you have to ask yourself why Microsoft would pay such an immense amount of money for a small Swedish company that owns just three games. Furthermore, the creative talent behind these games, founders Markus Persson, Jakob Porsér and Carl Manneh, were not included in the deal. All three announced they would leave the company with immediate effect.

The answer may lie in *Minecraft's* extraordinary community. "Some things that are special to us about *Minecraft* is the broad set of gamers that play this game," said Phil Spencer, the head of Xbox at Microsoft. "You have young and old, male and female. There's truly very few things in the market – whether games, movies, TV – like it."

This relationship between Mojang and its large, global community has huge potential for Microsoft, who will be able to promote their own products and those of other brands within *Minecraft*. This is powerful because this content will feel far more natural than traditional adverts, which are often ignored. A sequel to *Minecraft*, with enhanced graphics, might also go a long way to recouping the cost of buying Mojang, generating more revenue and prolonging the life of this unique community.

Whether this strategy will work is yet to be seen. Mojang allowed the *Minecraft* community to grow independently, with players being free to do whatever they like in the game. A large corporation like Microsoft may not be so liberal. One thing is for certain, however. People are not going to stop playing this amazing game any time soon.

Business Matters

Cross promotion

Cross promotion is a form of marketing in which one brand is attached to many different types of products. Its purpose is to raise the profile of the brand and to encourage its fans to buy the related product. An example of this is the virtual *Minecraft* T-shirts that were made available to download in the online game *Battlefield Heroes* in July 2011.

Market a new Minecraft product

When you create a fantastic new product, you need to come up with a marketing strategy to sell it. Here's a sample marketing strategy for a new *Minecraft* game. Why not see if you can come up with your own idea for a game, and think about how you would market it?

Minecraft 2

Minecraft is one of the most successful games of all time. It is known and loved by a huge global community of fans. Imagine you are leading the team at Microsoft tasked with launching a sequel, *Minecraft 2*. Put together a plan to market and promote the new game. You will need to think about the following:

1) CORPORATE OBJECTIVES

What do you want *Minecraft 2* to achieve? Do you just want to sell loads of copies of the new game or are you trying to sell other Microsoft products as well? You may want to ensure that *Minecraft 2* runs on all Microsoft products, from phones to laptops. Set a target of the number of games you want to sell in a year on each platform.

2) PRODUCT AND PRICE

How will *Minecraft 2* work and how will it be different from *Minecraft*? Will it have better graphics and new characters? Can you use what you know about *Minecraft* to add extra value to the new game, such as in-game YouTube links for tips and tricks? Write a description of gameplay in *Minecraft 2*. Remember, even small improvements will encourage fans to buy the new game.

Finally, how much will it cost? Will prices be different for mobile devices, and will you offer a discount for schools? You may even decide to offer a basic version of the game for free, and charge for mods.

3) PROTECT YOUR BRAND

Minecraft is an instantly recognizable brand with a unique approach to gaming. You will want to make sure *Minecraft's* massive fan base buys *Minecraft 2*, and this will mean keeping Mojang's sense of fun and creativity. Try to capture in a sentence what you think the spirit of *Minecraft* is. Then come up with an idea to bring the brand together with Microsoft's. For example, you could you make clever changes to the Microsoft logo to represent it in *Minecraft* blocks.

4) PROFILE YOUR CUSTOMERS

Children, adults and even teachers play *Minecraft*! You will need to create profiles of some of your potential customers – who are they, where do they live, do they play *Minecraft* alone on a tablet, or online with others? Do they buy merch or guides to the game? Identify and profile who you think your three best customers will be.

5) ANALYSE THE COMPETITON

The games market is highly competitive, so you will need to be aware of other games. If you can see someone is producing a game like yours, how will *Minecraft 2* be better? Select a game that *Minecraft* players might also like – are there popular elements you can take from it to incorporate into *Minecraft 2* to improve it? For example, players might like timed missions to play within *Minecraft 2*.

6) BUILD YOUR ADVERTISING CAMPAIGN

You will need some key advertising messages to bring the game alive in the press. Can you sum up the new game in a single killer sentence such as "*Minecraft 2*: The blocks are back in town"? What images will be on posters or advertisements? Try to design a poster to promote the new game.

Make a list of where you will display advertising. Will you buy space in magazines or on TV? *Minecraft* is an online phenomenon so you may want to create websites or run a campaign on social media websites such as YouTube and Facebook. Remember you also have existing Microsoft products to help you, so you could offer a demo of the new game with new Microsoft Office or Xbox products.

7) MAKE A SPLASH

The sequel to one of the most successful video games of all time is likely to make the news. But nothing gets sales going like a news story in the press. You have all the money and marketing power of Microsoft behind you so go to town and write a proposal for a launch event. Which celebrities might you invite and what would they do to catch headlines? Will you launch the new game to fans at Minecon?

Timing is key to the success of your launch, too, so think carefully about when would be best to do it. Will you try and capture some pre-Christmas sales on the high street, or release the game in time for the summer holidays?

glossary

8-bit
A reference to a generation of computers that used 8 units of data in instructions. Their programs were simple, and their graphics were square and blocky.

AB
An abbreviation of Aktiebolag, meaning a limited company.

App
A program designed to do a particular job.

Community
A group of people sharing an interest.

Console
A dedicated computer designed to run games. For example, a PlayStation or a Nintendo Wii.

End-User License Agreement (EULA)
A legal agreement between a games publisher and someone who uses their product governing the use of a game.

Hardware
The physical device on which a computer program is run.

Hack
A term used by developers to describe building or changing code or databases created by someone else.

Hackathon
A competitive event in which developers race to code a new game in a set period of time.

In-game
Features, advertisements, power ups or new products that are sold or delivered inside a game

License
The legal right granted to a company to use the brand of another company for commercial purposes.

Marketing
The activity of presenting, advertising and selling a company's products.

Minecon
A convention for *Minecraft* fans featuring events and exhibitions.

Minecraft Edu
Service that offers cheap licenses and tools to schools to use *Minecraft* as an educational tool.

Mods
Changes made to an original game such as adding more content.

Operating system
The code that underpins and supports the basic functions of a computer. Different OS might be used to run PCs, tablets and mobile devices.

PC
Personal computer.

Platform
The operating system of a device on which programs are run.

Proposal
A formal, written plan suggesting a course of action.

Rank
A package of services sold to a user when subscribing to a *Minecraft* server.

Revenue
The money a company earns from the sale of goods and services.

Server
Dedicated computer that is the home to websites online.

Software
The code that runs a computer's operating system or a program running on it.

Sponsor
A company that pays towards an event or project so that they can be associated with it.

YouTube
Website owned by Google that hosts short films.

further information

Books

Minecraft Blockopedia
(Egmont, 2014)

Minecraft Beginner's Handbook
(Egmont, 2013)

Minecraft Redstone Handbook
(Egmont, 2013)

Minecraft Combat Handbook
(Egmont, 2014)

Minecraft Construction Handbook
(Egmont, 2014)

Web

Minecraft
https://minecraft.net/

Mojang
https://mojang.com/

***Minecraft* Lego**
http://www.lego.com/en-gb/minecraft

First published in Great Britain in 2015 by Wayland

Copyright © Wayland, 2015

All rights reserved.
Dewey Number: 338.7'617948-dc23
ISBN: 978 0 7502 9252 8
Ebook ISBN: 978 0 7502 9253 5
10 9 8 7 6 5 4 3 2 1
Printed in China

Wayland
An imprint of Hachette Children's Group
Part of Hodder & Stoughton
Carmelite House
50 Victoria Embankment
London EC4Y 0DZ
An Hachette UK Company
www.hachette.co.uk

www.hachettechildrens.co.uk
Editor: Elizabeth Brent
Designer: Grant Kempster

Picture Credits: Cover: Caro/Photoshot (left), Kobby Dagan / Shutterstock.com (right); p4: Stefano Tinti/Shutterstock.com; p5: 1000 Words/Shutterstock.com; p6: Joe Raedle/Getty Images; p7: Chris Ratcliffe/Bloomberg via Getty Images (top); Shutterstock.com (bottom); p8: Pikawil/Wikicommons; p9: AcPA/TopFoto; p10: Photofusion/REX (top), OlegDoroshin/Shutterstock.com (bottom); p11: Anatolii Babii/Alamy; p12: Chris Ratcliffe/Bloomberg via Getty Images; p13: Chris Ratcliffe/Bloomberg via Getty Images (left), A© PA/TopFoto (right); p14: INTS KALNINS/Reuters/Corbis (top), FREDRIK SANDBERG/SCANPIX/TT News Agency/Press Association Images (bottom); p15 ROBERTO ZILLI/Shutterstock.com; p16: africa924/Shutterstock.com (top); Aleksandar Todorovic/Shutterstock.com (bottom); p17: Multiplay UK/Wikicommons; p18: OlegDoroshin/Shutterstock.com; p19: Tamisclao/Shutterstock.com; p20: A© PA/TopFoto; p21: Picture Alliance/Photoshot; p22: Smontgom65/Dreamstime.com; p23: Miles Willis/Getty Images for Ascot Racecourse; p24: Ingvar Bjork/Shutterstock.com; p25: Alberto E. Rodriguez/WireImage; p26: JStone/Shutterstock.com (inset), Jesse Knish/Getty Images for SXSW (bottom), Imagebroker/Photoshot (top); p28: Erik Tham/Demotix/Corbis

DISCOVER THE INCREDIBLE STORIES OF THE BUSINESSES BEHIND THESE WORLD-FAMOUS BRANDS

978 0 7502 9264 1

978 0 7502 9261 0

978 0 7502 9252 8

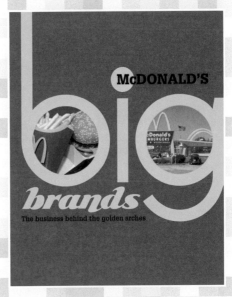

978 0 7502 9255 9